95 Things I Never Thought I'd Say or Hear Until I Had Kids

To order additional copies, please contact us.
BookSurge, LLC
www.booksurge.com
1-866-308-6235
orders@booksurge.com

B. L.
RITTER

95 THINGS I NEVER THOUGHT I'D SAY OR HEAR UNTIL I HAD KIDS

2005

95 Things I Never Thought I'd Say or Hear Until I Had Kids

To The Wonderful People In My Life That Said The Things To Make This Book Possible - My Boys Baden And Mason. And To My Husband, Brian, Who Ran With Me To The Other Room To Laugh When It Was Necessary. I Would Also Like To Thank Marcy Weavil, Who Did Such A Wonderful Job On My Cover. I Never Would Have Been Able To Do It Without Her.

1. Because I said so
2. No, you cannot look at your brother's poop
3. I guess your penis *is* kind of like a lion's tail, but please stop wagging it

4. Well, he'll poop it out eventually
5. Look how fat he is! That is so adorable!
6. Nobody is allowed to touch anybody anymore!

7.   Your underwear goes on *before* your pants

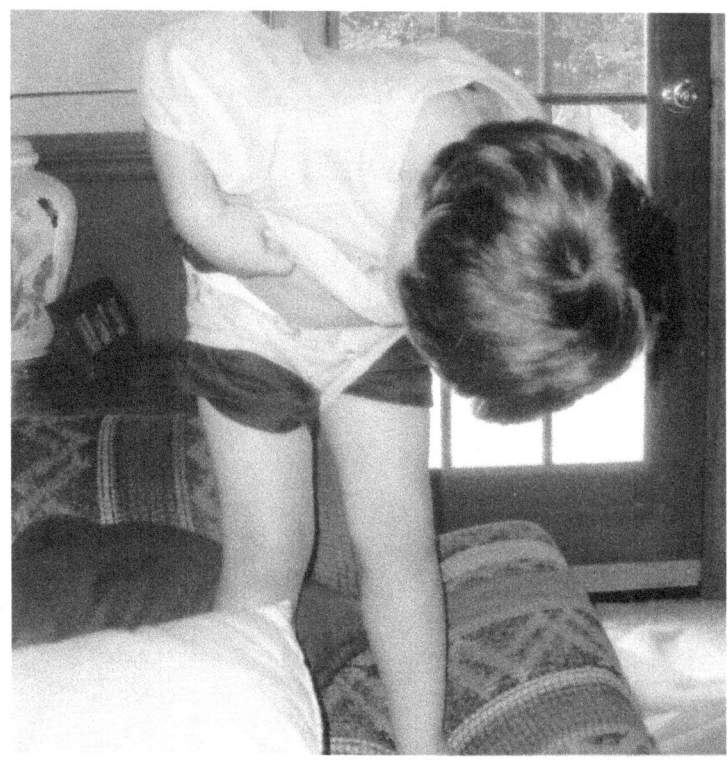

8. I don't know sweetie—what *does* your finger smell like?
9. Isn't that sweet—he's got hair on his back!
10. Stop touching my eye!

11. I don't care—as long as you don't do anything weird with it.
12. No I *don't* want to smell your finger after you've scratched your butt
13. It's not polite to touch yourself in public

14. Go smell (or let me go smell) his butt. I think he pooped.
15. Stop picking your nose! (This one could also be used on husbands)
16. If you put that up your nose, I'll have to dig it out and it's going to hurt

17. Just because there's a hole there doesn't mean you have to stick something in it
18. Don't *make* me tell you again!
19. From my son, "Chocolate milk will make me not be sad anymore."

20. Well just stop looking at each other then!

21. Don't run with that pencil! If you fall, you'll stab yourself in the face!
22. From my son, "Tell Mason not to gnaw on my arm!"
23. Please stop smelling your brother's diaper

24. The dog doesn't like to be colored on
25. Fish food is for fish—not you. You don't like it do you?
26. Don't sit too close to the TV. You're going to go blind.

27. Spiderman poops in the potty—don't you want to?
28. Please don't spit on me. I don't like it.
29. The first time my oldest son saw me breast feeding his brother, he started crying. When I asked him what was wrong he tearfully said, "Mason's eating mommy!"

30. Hey mommy—I'm a good pooper!
31. I don't want your finger up *my* nose either
32. My oldest son said, "When Mason grows up, I'm going to grow down."

33. You cannot go to the store naked
34. You are just like your father!
35. I bet you won't do that again now, will you?

36. I told my son I didn't have any money and he said,
    "But you do! Just get it out of the machine and put
    it in the cup like you do at Chuck E. Cheese!"
37. Just remember—I see and hear everything
38. Don't eat the candle! Ick!

39. We do not stick crayons in our ears
40. I'm not going to tell you again not to paint on the fish tank!
41. I'm your mother—I know everything

42. If you don't brush your teeth, they're going to fall out
43. I think somebody needs to go to timeout
44. I'm going to throw up if I ride the carousel one more time

45.   Don't stick your hand in the toilet!

46. No, you cannot ride the dog!
47. His poop was a little hard yesterday. What do you think?
48. You can watch the movie after your nap

49. At least when I'm at work I can go to the bathroom and eat when I want to!

50. Mommy got paid today—let's go to Chuck E. Cheese!

51. Yea! You can write your name!

52. Just wait until your father gets home
53. Do you want to watch Barney again?
54. Don't put that marble in your mouth!

55. You're right sweetie. Daddy doesn't have Spiderman on his underwear—only you do.
56. If you do it again, I'm going to spank you.
57. You just sit there and think about it for a minute

58. Let's talk about why you're in trouble

59. Why don't you ask me a little bit nicer?
60. Make sure you watch him. He might try to eat the cat.
61. Please don't eat my earrings.

62. If you would listen the first time, I wouldn't have to yell! (Of course, this could be used with a husband as well.)
63. Why do you make me yell at you?
64. If you don't eat, you'll never be like Spiderman

65. Go to your room!
66. Monsters aren't real—I promise.
67. Just give him a pot and a spoon. He'll be happy for hours

68. Hurry and get a picture of him eating the dirt
69. Pooping in the potty does not hurt
70. I told my son that we were going to go play in the kiddie corner and he asked me, "Are we in the doggie corner right now?" He thought I meant "Kitty Corner"

71. No, we're not there yet
72. If he jumped off a bridge, would you do it, too?
73. I don't care what they did on TV—you cannot shoot darts in people's necks!

74. Don't make me stop this car!
75. Don't eat the dog food
76. If you eat the book, we won't be able to read it anymore

77. We don't eat off of the floor
78. If you hit one more person with that baseball bat, it's going in the trash
79. You have a limit of asking "why" 10 times today

80. From my son yesterday, "Mommy, go sit on the couch so I can throw things at you."

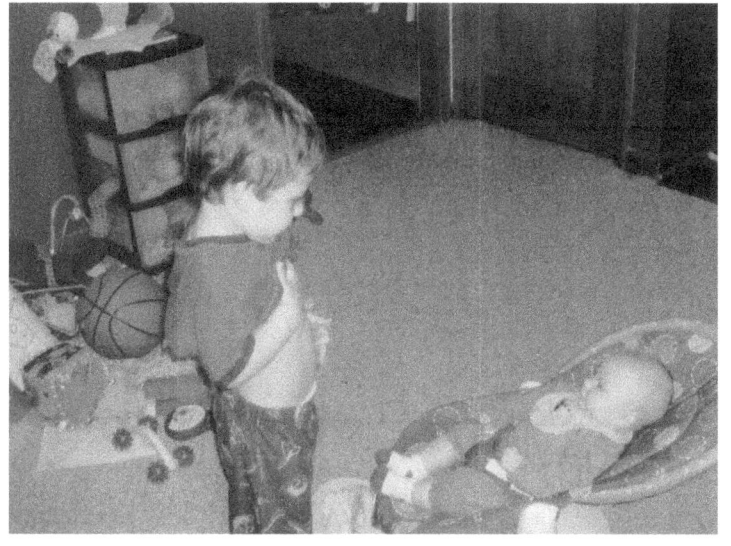

81. If you do it again, I'm going to tell your father!
82. I think its time I introduced you to the "sassy corner"
83. Did you just stick that tic tac up your nose?

84. Why did you stick that eraser in your ear?
85. (The response to the previous question) "Because you said I would choke if I stuck it in my mouth!"
86. I am sick and tired of this!

87. Look at this pig sty!
88. Please stop wiping your nose on me!
89. Stop playing kung-fu with the Lincoln logs—you're going to hurt somebody.

90. Look at him. I love it when they don't have any teeth.

91. He's so cute. I love it when they're bald!
92. We do not eat things out of the trash!
93. Mommy's body spray isn't *supposed* to clean windows

94. From my grandmother, "If you don't stop crying, I'm going to give you something to cry about!

95. Thank you for decorating the door, but stickers are supposed to go on paper

www.ingramcontent.com/pod-product-compliance
Lightning Source LLC
Chambersburg PA
CBHW070339290526
45791CB00003B/1389